WHAT IS WEATHER?

LOUISE SPILSBURY

Published in 2014 by Britannica Educational Publishing (a trademark of Encyclopædia Britannica, Inc.) in association with The Rosen Publishing Group, Inc.
29 East 21st Street, New York, NY 10010

Distributed exclusively by Rosen Publishing.
To see additional Britannica Educational Publishing titles, go to rosenpublishing.com

First Edition

Britannica Educational Publishing
J.E. Luebering: Director, Core Reference Group
Anthony L. Green: Editor, Compton's by Britannica

Rosen Publishing
Hope Lourie Killcoyne: Executive Editor
Nelson Sá: Art Director

Library of Congress Cataloging-in-Publication Data

Spilsbury, Louise, author.
What is weather?/Louise Spilsbury. — First edition.
        pages cm. — (Let's find out: earth science)
Includes bibliographical references and index.
ISBN 978-1-62275-276-8 (library binding) — ISBN 978-1-62275-279-9 (pbk.) — ISBN 978-1-62275-280-5 (6-pack)
1. Weather — Juvenile literature. 2. Climatology — Juvenile literature. I. Title.
QC981.3.S664 2014
551.6 — dc23
                                                                        2013023016

Manufactured in the United States of America

Photo credits
Cover: Shutterstock Pichugin Dmitry. Inside: Dreamstime: 7xpert 8–9, Bestfotos 11, Bridgetjones 23, Cta88 10, Darrenbaker 22, Darrengreen 25, Dbvirago 21, Flysnow 19, Iofoto 29, Lienkie 20, Lostarts 12, MatildeToscani 13, Mikeexpert 16, Tatiana Popova 27, Rmorijn 4–5, Sergey76 7, Snoozle 28, Solarseven 9, Staphy 26, Aleksey Stemmer 18, Thefinalmiracle 5, Trifff 6, Typhoonski 24–25, Zastavkin 14; Shutterstock: Pichugin Dmitry 1, Suzanne Tucker 15, Vvoe 17.

CONTENTS

WORLD OF WEATHER

Before you get dressed in the morning, do you see what the weather is going to be like? Weather is the state of the atmosphere at any given time and place. It has a huge effect on our lives. Heavy rain can spoil your plans for a day out. Cold weather can kill a farmer's plants. A sunny day can make people feel more cheerful.

▶▶ **Warm, dry weather helps fruit ripen and gives workers the chance to pick it.**

There are many different types of weather. The weather can be hot, cold, or somewhere in between. It can also be dry, humid or wet, sunny, partly cloudy, or gray.

Weather affects our lives in many ways, but what causes different types of weather?

Heavy rains can cause flooding.

THINK ABOUT IT

As you read this book, think about how different types of weather are connected. For example, how are sun and wind connected?

5

THE SUN

The sun is a star. A star is a giant ball of burning gas. The sun is the nearest star to Earth. Like other stars, the sun gives off huge amounts of heat and light **energy**. The sun is about 93 million miles (150 million km) from Earth, but still provides our planet with its heat and light!

The sun is the star at the center of our solar system.

Energy is power that can make things work, move, live, and grow.

THINK ABOUT IT
The light and heat from the sun are very strong. Why do you think people should wear sunblock on hot, sunny days?

The sun makes it warm enough for living things to survive on Earth. Plants use sunlight to make food and grow. People need plants to eat, and also to feed the animals that we eat. Without the sun, there would be no life at all on Earth!

THE ATMOSPHERE

The atmosphere is the blanket of gases that surrounds Earth. The atmosphere helps keep the world warm. When heat energy from the sun warms Earth's surface, the warm land heats the air above it. Warm air rises, so some heat escapes into space. The atmosphere also reflects heat back toward Earth, which helps to keep us warm.

THINK ABOUT IT

When people burn fuels, they put more gases into the atmosphere. What effect do you think this might have on the amount of heat the atmosphere traps on Earth?

▶▶ The atmosphere keeps our planet warm.

All of Earth's weather happens in the lowest part of the atmosphere, closest to Earth. This layer of air can be wet, dry, hot, cold, moving, or still. The changes in this layer of the atmosphere give us our many different types of weather.

The weight of the air above a given area is called atmospheric pressure. Changes in pressure help people to predict approaching storms. (A storm is a disturbance in the atmosphere—for example, a thunderstorm or hurricane.)

Clouds

Clouds form when the sun warms Earth's surface. Heat from the ground then warms the air just above it. When warm air rises and moves high up in the sky, it cools down again. This turns the **water vapor** in the air back into tiny drops of water. These drops of water collect together and form clouds.

These are cumulus clouds. They are dense, puffy clouds.

Water vapor is the gas that forms in air when water is warm.

Dark clouds such as these mean that rain is on the way.

The three main types of clouds are cirrus, cumulus, and stratus. Cirrus clouds are high, thin clouds made up of ice crystals. Cumulus clouds are puffy clouds that are often piled up like mountains. Stratus clouds are flat layers of clouds. Nimbus is the latin word for rain. A cumulonimbus cloud is a type of raincloud.

RAIN

Clouds often bring rain. Rain is a part of Earth's endless water cycle. At the beginning of the cycle, sunlight heats up water on Earth's surface. The heat causes the water to evaporate, or turn into water vapor. This water vapor rises into the air. As the water vapor cools, it turns back into water, in the form of droplets.

Rain is one form of precipitation. Other forms include hail, sleet, and snow.

THINK ABOUT IT

Why do you usually see rainbows after it rains?

Rainbows form when light from the sun comes into contact with tiny drops of water in the air. Sunlight looks clear, but it is made up of different colors. When sunlight passes through the droplets, the water bends the light and splits it into different colors.

You usually see seven colors in a rainbow.

Snow and Hail

Snow forms when the temperature of the sky is so cold that the water vapor in a cloud freezes. It turns from liquid water into tiny pieces of solid ice. The pieces of ice stick together and form snowflakes. When they become big and heavy, they fall from the sky.

> **Temperature** is how hot or cold something is.

> ▶▶ If the temperature on the ground is cold, snow does not melt when it lands.

Hail forms in giant cumulonimbus clouds. Fast winds in these clouds blow raindrops up into the top layers of the clouds. There, the air is so cold that it turns the raindrops into small balls of ice, called hailstones. They swirl around in the cloud, bump into each other, and join together. When they become too heavy to float, they fall to the ground.

Some hailstones are big and heavy. They can cause damage when they hit things on land.

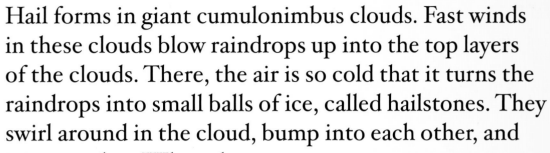

THUNDER AND LIGHTNING

Thunder and lightning come from cumulonimbus clouds, as well. These huge, dark clouds can reach from the ground to high in the sky. Winds blow tiny pieces of ice around in the clouds. When the pieces of ice rub against each other, they cause **static electricity**. If the electricity in the clouds builds up, it can cause a flash of lightning.

Lightning is an enormous spark of electricity between a cloud and the ground.

Lightning is very, very hot. As it travels through the air, it makes the air around it hot, too. This makes the air expand suddenly, which causes the loud bang that we call thunder.

If lightning hits a building, it can cause a fire. Today, many buildings have lightning rods. They carry the electricity from a lightning strike safely into the ground. This stops the lightning from setting the building on fire.

Lightning rod

Static electricity is a type of electricity caused by things rubbing together.

FROST AND DEW

Frost and dew form in the morning after a night during which the air has been cold and the sky clear. On nights such as this, the land gets colder than the air above it.

Frost forms when water vapor near the ground comes into contact with very cold surfaces. The water vapor turns into tiny pieces of ice.

Frost can damage plants if it freezes the water inside their leaves.

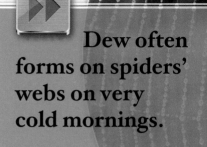

Dew often forms on spiders' webs on very cold mornings.

Dew forms on nights when the air near the ground is full of water vapor. When the temperature drops at night, water vapor in the air becomes cold, and turns into drops of water. These drops of water are near to the ground, so they often gather on surfaces, such as grass.

COMPARE AND CONTRAST
How are frost and dew similar? How are they different?

Mist and Fog

Mist and fog occur when the air is humid, or full of moisture, making tiny drops of water float in the air near Earth's surface. When water vapor just above the ground or over the sea meets a layer of cold air, the water vapor turns into tiny droplets of water. The droplets stay so small that they are light enough to float in the air. When fog is so thin that we can see through it, it is called mist.

Mist is thinner than fog because it contains fewer drops of water.

In thick fog, aircraft do not take off because pilots cannot see where they are going.

Fog is thicker than mist, and it can be dangerous. Fog can make it difficult for drivers to see where they are going, at night when it is also dark.

Both fog and mist are more likely to occur in warm weather, since warm air can hold more moisture than cold air can.

COMPARE AND CONTRAST

How are fog and mist similar to rain? How are they different?

WIND

Wind is moving air. Air moves because heat from the sun creates different temperatures. Sunlight warms the ground and then the air above the ground becomes warmer. When warm air rises, cool air moves in to fill the space the warm air has left behind. As the warm air rises, it gets cooler and sinks again. This moving air is wind. Winds may be gentle or powerful.

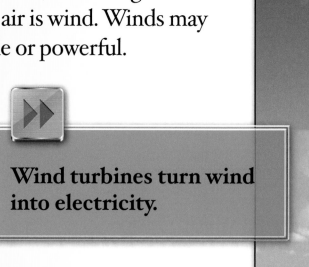

Wind turbines turn wind into electricity.

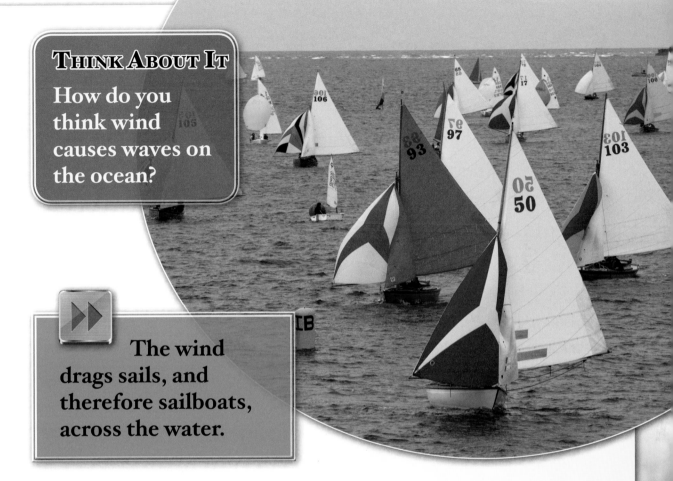

THINK ABOUT IT

How do you think wind causes waves on the ocean?

The wind drags sails, and therefore sailboats, across the water.

Areas of land, such as streets and fields, heat up faster in the sun than water does. That is why it is usually cooler at the coast than it is inland. When warm air above land rises, cooler air from the sea blows in to fill the space that the warm air leaves behind. This makes a cool sea breeze.

Seasons

Seasons are times of the year when the weather changes. Seasons change because Earth moves around the sun every year. This means that different parts of the planet get closer to the sun at different times of the year. For example, between March and August, the United States is closer to the sun, so this is when the country has its warm spring and summer seasons.

COMPARE AND CONTRAST

How do trees and plants look in spring and summer? How do they look in fall and winter?

▶▶ **People often enjoy the summer sun in New York City's Central Park.**

24

Many leaves change color in fall, before dropping off trees by winter.

The changing seasons bring changes to plants and animal life. In summer, there are more hours of sunlight, so this is when plants grow the most. In winter, there are fewer hours of sunlight, so some plants die. They grow again in spring.

DIFFERENT CLIMATES

Climate is the usual type of weather in a particular place. A country's climate tells you how hot, cold, wet, or snowy it is likely to be there at different times of the year. For example, a region may have cold winters and hot, dry summers. In some places, the climate stays the same all year. For example, deserts are always dry and Antarctica is always cold.

Penguins have a thick layer of fat to keep them warm in the freezing climate of Antarctica.

The usual temperatures of a place depend on the place's position on Earth. For example, the area around the equator is always hot. Our planet is shaped like a ball, but the sun's light and heat energy travel to Earth in a straight line. This means the energy strikes the equator directly, making it the hottest place on Earth.

The **equator** is an imaginary line around the middle of Earth.

Places near the equator are hot and sunny.

CHANGING CLIMATES

World climates change over thousands or millions of years. Today, however, our climate is changing very quickly. When people burn fuels such as coal, oil, and natural gas in engines and power stations, a gas called carbon dioxide is released. The gas escapes into the air, and then into the atmosphere. There, it traps more heat on Earth. This is making Earth hotter and hotter.

Power stations burn fuel such as coal to make electricity.

Riding your bike to school reduces the amount of fuel used in cars and buses.

THINK ABOUT IT

What can you do to slow down climate change?

Higher temperatures on Earth cause more extreme weather. There are more forest fires. Droughts cause plants to die because they do not have enough water. Stronger storms cause floods and blow down trees, damaging buildings. People are now trying to slow climate change, for example, by making electricity using the power of wind or sun instead of burning fuels.

Glossary

Antarctica The very cold region around Earth's South Pole.

atmosphere The blanket of gases that surrounds Earth.

carbon dioxide A colorless, odorless gas found in the atmosphere.

cirrus A high, thin, white cloud made up of tiny ice crystals.

climate The usual type of weather that a particular place experiences.

cumulonimbus A type of cloud that usually brings thunderstorms.

cumulus A dense, puffy cloud that has a flat base and rounded top.

deserts Dry areas of land that get little rain.

droplet A very small drop of water.

droughts Long periods of dry weather.

evaporate To turn from liquid into vapor.

freezes When a liquid, such as water, turns into ice.

fuels Substances, such as coal and natural gas, that people use to release heat.

gas A substance that floats in the air.

hail Small lumps of ice that fall from clouds, sometimes during thunderstorms.

humid Damp or moist.

ice The solid form of water.

lightning A giant spark of electricity between a cloud and the ground.

precipitation The liquid and solid water particles that fall from clouds and reach the ground.

reflects Bounces back.

seasons Certain times of the year, such as spring or fall.

sleet Frozen or partly frozen rain.

stratus A flat, layered cloud that covers a large area.

vapor Fine particles of matter, such as fog, floating in the air.

wind turbines Devices that convert energy from the wind into electricity.

FOR MORE INFORMATION

Books

Gosman, Gillian. *What Do You Know About Weather and Climate?* (20 Questions: Earth Science). New York, NY: Powerkids Press, 2013.

Kerrod, Robin. *Weather—An Amazing Fact File And Hands-On Project Book* (Exploring Science). North Wales, PA: Armadillo, 2013.

Rissman, Rebecca. *Seasons* (Picture This!). North Mankato, MN: Raintree, 2013.

Simon, Seymour. *Weather*. New York, NY: Harper Collins, 2006.

Weather (Eye Wonder). New York, NY: DK Publishing, 2004.

Websites

Due to the changing nature of Internet links, Rosen Publishing has developed an online list of Websites related to the subject of this book. This site is updated regularly. Please use this link to access the list:

http://www.rosenlinks.com/lfo/weat

INDEX